WEEKLY PLANNER

Thos book belongs to.. _____

Ok let me pencil you in.

2020

January

S	M	T	W	T	F	S
			1	2	3	4
5	6	7	8	9	10	11
12	13	14	15	16	17	18
19	20	21	22	23	24	25
26	27	28	29	30	31	

February

S	M	T	W	T	F	S
						1
2	3	4	5	6	7	8
9	10	11	12	13	14	15
16	17	18	19	20	21	22
23	24	25	26	27	28	29

March

S	M	T	W	T	F	S
1	2	3	4	5	6	7
8	9	10	11	12	13	14
15	16	17	18	19	20	21
22	23	24	25	26	27	28
29	30	31				

April

S	M	T	W	T	F	S
			1	2	3	4
5	6	7	8	9	10	11
12	13	14	15	16	17	18
19	20	21	22	23	24	25
26	27	28	29	30		

May

S	M	T	W	T	F	S
					1	2
3	4	5	6	7	8	9
10	11	12	13	14	15	16
17	18	19	20	21	22	23
24	25	26	27	28	29	30
31						

June

S	M	T	W	T	F	S
	1	2	3	4	5	6
7	8	9	10	11	12	13
14	15	16	17	18	19	20
21	22	23	24	25	26	27
28	29	30				

July

S	M	T	W	T	F	S
			1	2	3	4
5	6	7	8	9	10	11
12	13	14	15	16	17	18
19	20	21	22	23	24	25
26	27	28	29	30	31	

August

S	M	T	W	T	F	S
						1
2	3	4	5	6	7	8
9	10	11	12	13	14	15
16	17	18	19	20	21	22
23	24	25	26	27	28	29
30	31					

September

S	M	T	W	T	F	S
		1	2	3	4	5
6	7	8	9	10	11	12
13	14	15	16	17	18	19
20	21	22	23	24	25	26
27	28	29	30			

October

S	M	T	W	T	F	S
				1	2	3
4	5	6	7	8	9	10
11	12	13	14	15	16	17
18	19	20	21	22	23	24
25	26	27	28	29	30	31

November

S	M	T	W	T	F	S
1	2	3	4	5	6	7
8	9	10	11	12	13	14
15	16	17	18	19	20	21
22	23	24	25	26	27	28
29	30					

December

S	M	T	W	T	F	S
		1	2	3	4	5
6	7	8	9	10	11	12
13	14	15	16	17	18	19
20	21	22	23	24	25	26
27	28	29	30	31		

December

12/30/19 - 01/05/20

○ 30. MONDAY

3 THINGS I AM GRATEFUL FOR.

_____
_____
_____

○ 31. TUESDAY

_____
_____
_____
_____

○ 1. WEDNESDAY

WEEKLY GOALS

_____
_____
_____

○ 2. THURSDAY

_____
_____
_____
_____

○ 3. FRIDAY

_____
_____
_____
_____

○ 4. SATURDAY / 5. SUNDAY

_____
_____
_____

January

○ 6. MONDAY

3 THINGS I AM GRATEFUL FOR.

○ 7. TUESDAY

○ 8. WEDNESDAY

WEEKLY GOALS

○ 9. THURSDAY

○ 10. FRIDAY

○ 11. SATURDAY / 12. SUNDAY

January

01/13/20 - 01/19/20

○ 13. MONDAY

3 THINGS I AM GRATEFUL FOR.

_____
_____
_____

○ 14. TUESDAY

_____
_____
_____
_____

○ 15. WEDNESDAY

WEEKLY GOALS

_____
_____
_____

○ 16. THURSDAY

_____
_____
_____
_____

○ 17. FRIDAY

_____
_____
_____
_____

○ 18. SATURDAY / 19. SUNDAY

_____
_____
_____
_____

January

○ 20. MONDAY

3 THINGS I AM GRATEFUL FOR.

_____
_____
_____
_____
_____
_____
_____

○ 21. TUESDAY

○ 22. WEDNESDAY

WEEKLY GOALS

_____
_____
_____
_____
_____
_____
_____

○ 23. THURSDAY

_____
_____
_____
_____

○ 24. FRIDAY

_____
_____
_____
_____

○ 25. SATURDAY / 26. SUNDAY

_____
_____
_____

JANUARY

01/27/20 - 02/02/20

○ 27. MONDAY

3 THINGS I AM GRATEFUL FOR.

_____
_____
_____

○ 28. TUESDAY

_____
_____
_____
_____

○ 29. WEDNESDAY

WEEKLY GOALS

_____
_____

○ 30. THURSDAY

_____
_____
_____
_____
_____
_____

○ 31. FRIDAY

_____
_____
_____
_____

○ 1. SATURDAY / 2. SUNDAY

_____
_____
_____
_____

February

02/03/20 - 02/09/20

○ 3. MONDAY

3 THINGS I AM GRATEFUL FOR.

○ 4. TUESDAY

○ 5. WEDNESDAY

WEEKLY GOALS

○ 6. THURSDAY

○ 7. FRIDAY

○ 8. SATURDAY / 9. SUNDAY

February

○ 10. MONDAY

3 THINGS I AM GRATEFUL FOR.

○ 11. TUESDAY

○ 12. WEDNESDAY

WEEKLY GOALS

○ 13. THURSDAY

○ 14. FRIDAY

○ 15. SATURDAY / 16. SUNDAY

February

○ 17. MONDAY

3 THINGS I AM GRATEFUL FOR.

○ 18. TUESDAY

○ 19. WEDNESDAY

WEEKLY GOALS

○ 20. THURSDAY

○ 21. FRIDAY

○ 22. SATURDAY / 23. SUNDAY

FEBRUARY

02/24/20 - 03/01/20

○ 24. MONDAY

3 THINGS I AM GRATEFUL FOR.

_____
_____
_____
_____

○ 25. TUESDAY

_____
_____
_____

○ 26. WEDNESDAY

WEEKLY GOALS

_____
_____
_____
_____

○ 27. THURSDAY

_____
_____
_____
_____

○ 28. FRIDAY

_____
_____
_____
_____

○ 29. SATURDAY / 1. SUNDAY

_____
_____
_____

MARCH

         03/02/20 - 03/08/20

○ 2. MONDAY

3 THINGS I AM GRATEFUL FOR.

_____
_____
_____
_____
_____
_____
_____

○ 3. TUESDAY

○ 4. WEDNESDAY

WEEKLY GOALS

_____
_____
_____
_____
_____
_____
_____
_____

○ 5. THURSDAY

○ 6. FRIDAY

_____
_____
_____
_____

○ 7. SATURDAY / 8. SUNDAY

_____
_____
_____

MARCH

○ 9. MONDAY

3 THINGS I AM GRATEFUL FOR.

_____
_____
_____
_____

○ 10. TUESDAY

_____
_____
_____
_____

○ 11. WEDNESDAY

WEEKLY GOALS

_____
_____
_____

○ 12. THURSDAY

_____
_____
_____
_____

○ 13. FRIDAY

_____
_____
_____
_____

○ 14. SATURDAY / 15. SUNDAY

_____
_____
_____
_____

March

○ 16. MONDAY

3 THINGS I AM GRATEFUL FOR.

_____

_____

_____

○ 17. TUESDAY

_____

_____

_____

_____

○ 18. WEDNESDAY

WEEKLY GOALS

_____

_____

_____

○ 19. THURSDAY

_____

_____

_____

_____

_____

_____

○ 20. FRIDAY

_____

_____

_____

_____

_____

○ 21. SATURDAY / 22. SUNDAY

_____

_____

_____

_____

MARCH

03/23/20 - 03/29/20

○ 23. MONDAY

3 THINGS I AM GRATEFUL FOR.

_____
_____
_____
_____

○ 24. TUESDAY

_____
_____
_____
_____

○ 25. WEDNESDAY

WEEKLY GOALS

_____
_____
_____
_____

○ 26. THURSDAY

_____
_____
_____
_____

○ 27. FRIDAY

_____
_____
_____
_____

○ 28. SATURDAY / 29. SUNDAY

_____
_____
_____
_____

MARCH

○ 30. MONDAY

3 THINGS I AM GRATEFUL FOR.

○ 31. TUESDAY

○ 1. WEDNESDAY

WEEKLY GOALS

○ 2. THURSDAY

○ 3. FRIDAY

○ 4. SATURDAY / 5. SUNDAY

APRIL

○ 6. MONDAY

3 THINGS I AM GRATEFUL FOR.

_____

_____

_____

○ 7. TUESDAY

_____

_____

_____

_____

○ 8. WEDNESDAY

WEEKLY GOALS

_____

_____

_____

_____

○ 9. THURSDAY

_____

_____

_____

_____

_____

○ 10. FRIDAY

_____

_____

_____

_____

_____

○ 11. SATURDAY / 12. SUNDAY

_____

_____

_____

_____

APRIL

04/13/20 - 04/19/20

○ 13. MONDAY

3 THINGS I AM GRATEFUL FOR.

○ 14. TUESDAY

○ 15. WEDNESDAY

WEEKLY GOALS

○ 16. THURSDAY

○ 17. FRIDAY

○ 18. SATURDAY / 19. SUNDAY

APRIL

○ 20. MONDAY

3 THINGS I AM GRATEFUL FOR.

○ 21. TUESDAY

○ 22. WEDNESDAY

WEEKLY GOALS

○ 23. THURSDAY

○ 24. FRIDAY

○ 25. SATURDAY / 26. SUNDAY

APRIL

04/27/20 - 05/03/20

○ 27. MONDAY

3 THINGS I AM GRATEFUL FOR.

_____
_____
_____
_____

○ 28. TUESDAY

_____
_____
_____

○ 29. WEDNESDAY

WEEKLY GOALS

_____
_____
_____

○ 30. THURSDAY

_____
_____
_____
_____

○ 1. FRIDAY

_____
_____
_____
_____
_____

○ 2. SATURDAY / 3. SUNDAY

_____
_____
_____
_____
_____

MAY

05/04/20 - 05/10/20

○ 4. MONDAY

3 THINGS I AM GRATEFUL FOR.

○ 5. TUESDAY

○ 6. WEDNESDAY

WEEKLY GOALS

○ 7. THURSDAY

○ 8. FRIDAY

○ 9. SATURDAY / 10. SUNDAY

MAY

○ 11. MONDAY

3 THINGS I AM GRATEFUL FOR.

○ 12. TUESDAY

○ 13. WEDNESDAY

WEEKLY GOALS

○ 14. THURSDAY

○ 15. FRIDAY

○ 16. SATURDAY / 17. SUNDAY

MAY

05/18/20 - 05/24/20

○ 18. MONDAY

3 THINGS I AM GRATEFUL FOR.

_____

_____

_____

○ 19. TUESDAY

_____

_____

_____

_____

_____

○ 20. WEDNESDAY

WEEKLY GOALS

_____

_____

_____

_____

○ 21. THURSDAY

_____

_____

_____

_____

_____

○ 22. FRIDAY

_____

_____

_____

_____

○ 23. SATURDAY / 24. SUNDAY

_____

_____

_____

_____

MAY

05/25/20 - 05/31/20

○ 25. MONDAY

3 THINGS I AM GRATEFUL FOR.

○ 26. TUESDAY

○ 27. WEDNESDAY

WEEKLY GOALS

○ 28. THURSDAY

○ 29. FRIDAY

○ 30. SATURDAY / 31. SUNDAY

JUNE

06/01/20 - 06/07/20

○ 1. MONDAY

3 THINGS I AM GRATEFUL FOR.

_____
_____
_____

○ 2. TUESDAY

_____
_____
_____
_____

○ 3. WEDNESDAY

WEEKLY GOALS

_____
_____
_____

○ 4. THURSDAY

_____
_____
_____
_____
_____

○ 5. FRIDAY

_____
_____
_____
_____

○ 6. SATURDAY / 7. SUNDAY

_____
_____
_____
_____

JUNE

06/08/20 - 06/14/20

○ 8. MONDAY

3 THINGS I AM GRATEFUL FOR.

○ 9. TUESDAY

○ 10. WEDNESDAY

WEEKLY GOALS

○ 11. THURSDAY

○ 12. FRIDAY

○ 13. SATURDAY / 14. SUNDAY

JUNE

WEEK 25

06/15/20 - 06/21/20

○ 15. MONDAY

3 THINGS I AM GRATEFUL FOR.

○ 16. TUESDAY

○ 17. WEDNESDAY

WEEKLY GOALS

○ 18. THURSDAY

○ 19. FRIDAY

○ 20. SATURDAY / 21. SUNDAY

JUNE

06/22/20 - 06/28/20

○ 22. MONDAY

3 THINGS I AM GRATEFUL FOR.

_____
_____
_____
_____
_____
_____
_____
_____

○ 23. TUESDAY

○ 24. WEDNESDAY

WEEKLY GOALS

_____
_____
_____
_____
_____
_____

○ 25. THURSDAY

_____
_____
_____
_____
_____

○ 26. FRIDAY

_____
_____
_____
_____
_____

○ 27. SATURDAY / 28. SUNDAY

_____
_____
_____

JUNE

06/29/20 - 07/05/20

○ 29. MONDAY

3 THINGS I AM GRATEFUL FOR.

○ 30. TUESDAY

○ 1. WEDNESDAY

WEEKLY GOALS

○ 2. THURSDAY

○ 3. FRIDAY

○ 4. SATURDAY / 5. SUNDAY

JULY

07/06/20 - 07/12/20

○ 6. MONDAY

3 THINGS I AM GRATEFUL FOR.

○ 7. TUESDAY

○ 8. WEDNESDAY

WEEKLY GOALS

○ 9. THURSDAY

○ 10. FRIDAY

○ 11. SATURDAY / 12. SUNDAY

JULY

07/13/20 - 07/19/20

○ 13. MONDAY

3 THINGS I AM GRATEFUL FOR.

_____

_____

_____

○ 14. TUESDAY

_____

_____

_____

_____

_____

○ 15. WEDNESDAY

WEEKLY GOALS

_____

_____

_____

○ 16. THURSDAY

_____

_____

_____

_____

_____

○ 17. FRIDAY

_____

_____

_____

_____

_____

○ 18. SATURDAY / 19. SUNDAY

_____

_____

_____

_____

JULY

07/20/20 - 07/26/20

○ 20. MONDAY

3 THINGS I AM GRATEFUL FOR.

_____

_____

_____

○ 21. TUESDAY

_____

_____

_____

_____

○ 22. WEDNESDAY

WEEKLY GOALS

_____

_____

_____

○ 23. THURSDAY

_____

_____

_____

_____

○ 24. FRIDAY

_____

_____

_____

_____

○ 25. SATURDAY / 26. SUNDAY

_____

_____

_____

_____

_____

JULY

07/27/20 - 08/02/20

○ 27. MONDAY

3 THINGS I AM GRATEFUL FOR.

○ 28. TUESDAY

○ 29. WEDNESDAY

WEEKLY GOALS

○ 30. THURSDAY

○ 31. FRIDAY

○ 1. SATURDAY / 2. SUNDAY

AUGUST

08/03/20 - 08/09/20

○ 3. MONDAY

3 THINGS I AM GRATEFUL FOR.

_____
_____
_____

○ 4. TUESDAY

_____
_____
_____
_____

○ 5. WEDNESDAY

WEEKLY GOALS

_____
_____
_____

○ 6. THURSDAY

_____
_____
_____
_____

○ 7. FRIDAY

_____
_____
_____
_____

○ 8. SATURDAY / 9. SUNDAY

_____
_____
_____

AUGUST

○ 10. MONDAY

3 THINGS I AM GRATEFUL FOR.

○ 11. TUESDAY

○ 12. WEDNESDAY

WEEKLY GOALS

○ 13. THURSDAY

○ 14. FRIDAY

○ 15. SATURDAY / 16. SUNDAY

AUGUST

08/17/20 - 08/23/20

○ 17. MONDAY

3 THINGS I AM GRATEFUL FOR.

_____

_____

_____

○ 18. TUESDAY

_____

_____

_____

_____

○ 19. WEDNESDAY

WEEKLY GOALS

_____

_____

_____

○ 20. THURSDAY

_____

_____

_____

_____

_____

○ 21. FRIDAY

_____

_____

_____

_____

_____

○ 22. SATURDAY / 23. SUNDAY

_____

_____

_____

_____

AUGUST

08/24/20 - 08/30/20

○ 24. MONDAY

                                       3 THINGS I AM GRATEFUL FOR.

                    _____

                    _____

○ 25. TUESDAY

                    _____

                    _____

                    _____

○ 26. WEDNESDAY

                    WEEKLY GOALS

                    _____

○ 27. THURSDAY

                    _____

                    _____

○ 28. FRIDAY

                    _____

                    _____

○ 29. SATURDAY / 30. SUNDAY

                    _____

                    _____

AUGUST

08/31/20 - 09/06/20

○ 31. MONDAY

3 THINGS I AM GRATEFUL FOR.

_____

_____

○ 1. TUESDAY

_____

_____

_____

_____

_____

○ 2. WEDNESDAY

WEEKLY GOALS

_____

_____

_____

○ 3. THURSDAY

_____

_____

_____

_____

○ 4. FRIDAY

_____

_____

_____

_____

_____

○ 5. SATURDAY / 6. SUNDAY

_____

_____

_____

_____

September

○ 7. MONDAY

3 THINGS I AM GRATEFUL FOR.

_____
_____
_____

○ 8. TUESDAY

_____
_____
_____

○ 9. WEDNESDAY

WEEKLY GOALS

_____
_____

○ 10. THURSDAY

_____
_____
_____
_____

○ 11. FRIDAY

_____
_____
_____
_____

○ 12. SATURDAY / 13. SUNDAY

_____
_____
_____
_____

September

○ 14. MONDAY

3 THINGS I AM GRATEFUL FOR.

○ 15. TUESDAY

○ 16. WEDNESDAY

WEEKLY GOALS

○ 17. THURSDAY

○ 18. FRIDAY

○ 19. SATURDAY / 20. SUNDAY

September

○ 21. MONDAY

3 THINGS I AM GRATEFUL FOR.

_____
_____
_____

○ 22. TUESDAY

_____
_____
_____

○ 23. WEDNESDAY

WEEKLY GOALS

_____
_____
_____

○ 24. THURSDAY

_____
_____
_____
_____

○ 25. FRIDAY

_____
_____
_____

○ 26. SATURDAY / 27. SUNDAY

_____
_____
_____

September

○ 28. MONDAY

3 THINGS I AM GRATEFUL FOR.

○ 29. TUESDAY

○ 30. WEDNESDAY

WEEKLY GOALS

○ 1. THURSDAY

○ 2. FRIDAY

○ 3. SATURDAY / 4. SUNDAY

OCTOBER

○ 5. MONDAY

3 THINGS I AM GRATEFUL FOR.

○ 6. TUESDAY

○ 7. WEDNESDAY

WEEKLY GOALS

○ 8. THURSDAY

○ 9. FRIDAY

○ 10. SATURDAY / 11. SUNDAY

OCTOBER

○ 12. MONDAY

3 THINGS I AM GRATEFUL FOR.

○ 13. TUESDAY

○ 14. WEDNESDAY

WEEKLY GOALS

○ 15. THURSDAY

○ 16. FRIDAY

○ 17. SATURDAY / 18. SUNDAY

OCTOBER

10/19/20 - 10/25/20

○ 19. MONDAY

3 THINGS I AM GRATEFUL FOR.

○ 20. TUESDAY

○ 21. WEDNESDAY

WEEKLY GOALS

○ 22. THURSDAY

○ 23. FRIDAY

○ 24. SATURDAY / 25. SUNDAY

October

○ 26. MONDAY

3 THINGS I AM GRATEFUL FOR.

○ 27. TUESDAY

○ 28. WEDNESDAY

WEEKLY GOALS

○ 29. THURSDAY

○ 30. FRIDAY

○ 31. SATURDAY / 1. SUNDAY

November

○ 2. MONDAY

3 THINGS I AM GRATEFUL FOR.

_____

_____

_____

_____

○ 3. TUESDAY

_____

_____

_____

_____

○ 4. WEDNESDAY

WEEKLY GOALS

_____

_____

_____

○ 5. THURSDAY

_____

_____

_____

_____

○ 6. FRIDAY

_____

_____

_____

_____

○ 7. SATURDAY / 8. SUNDAY

_____

_____

_____

_____

November

○ 9. MONDAY

3 THINGS I AM GRATEFUL FOR.

○ 10. TUESDAY

○ 11. WEDNESDAY

WEEKLY GOALS

○ 12. THURSDAY

○ 13. FRIDAY

○ 14. SATURDAY / 15. SUNDAY

November

WEEK 47   11/16/20 - 11/22/20

○ 16. MONDAY

3 THINGS I AM GRATEFUL FOR.

_____
_____
_____
_____

○ 17. TUESDAY

_____
_____
_____

○ 18. WEDNESDAY

WEEKLY GOALS

_____
_____
_____

○ 19. THURSDAY

_____
_____
_____
_____
_____

○ 20. FRIDAY

_____
_____
_____
_____
_____

○ 21. SATURDAY / 22. SUNDAY

_____
_____
_____
_____

November

○ 23. MONDAY

3 THINGS I AM GRATEFUL FOR.

○ 24. TUESDAY

○ 25. WEDNESDAY

WEEKLY GOALS

○ 26. THURSDAY

○ 27. FRIDAY

○ 28. SATURDAY / 29. SUNDAY

November

○ 30. MONDAY

3 THINGS I AM GRATEFUL FOR.

○ 1. TUESDAY

○ 2. WEDNESDAY

WEEKLY GOALS

○ 3. THURSDAY

○ 4. FRIDAY

○ 5. SATURDAY / 6. SUNDAY

December

12/07/20 - 12/13/20

○ 7. MONDAY

3 THINGS I AM GRATEFUL FOR.

○ 8. TUESDAY

○ 9. WEDNESDAY

WEEKLY GOALS

○ 10. THURSDAY

○ 11. FRIDAY

○ 12. SATURDAY / 13. SUNDAY

DECEMBER

12/14/20 - 12/20/20

○ 14. MONDAY

3 THINGS I AM GRATEFUL FOR.

_____

_____

○ 15. TUESDAY

_____

_____

_____

_____

_____

○ 16. WEDNESDAY

WEEKLY GOALS

_____

_____

○ 17. THURSDAY

_____

_____

_____

_____

○ 18. FRIDAY

_____

_____

_____

○ 19. SATURDAY / 20. SUNDAY

_____

_____

_____

_____

December

○ 21. MONDAY

3 THINGS I AM GRATEFUL FOR.

_____
_____
_____
_____
_____
_____
_____

○ 22. TUESDAY

○ 23. WEDNESDAY

WEEKLY GOALS

_____
_____
_____
_____
_____
_____
_____

○ 24. THURSDAY

○ 25. FRIDAY

_____
_____
_____
_____
_____

○ 26. SATURDAY / 27. SUNDAY

_____
_____
_____

December

12/28/20 - 01/03/21

○ 28. MONDAY

3 THINGS I AM GRATEFUL FOR.

○ 29. TUESDAY

○ 30. WEDNESDAY

WEEKLY GOALS

○ 31. THURSDAY

○ 1. FRIDAY

○ 2. SATURDAY / 3. SUNDAY

Made in the USA
Las Vegas, NV
11 December 2022